Praise for *Seeds of Wisdom* & Joey O

"When somebody said, 'Listen to your mother,' Joey O paid attention. This inspirational book is the wonderful end result of that, passing along to its readers thoughtful guidance for their everyday lives."

—Arnold Palmer

". . . very entertaining . . . kind of you to think of me and I am most appreciative. I hope your career continues to go well. Very best wishes."

—Ben Hogan

"The power of love that Joey O has for his mother and her teachings has 'turbo charged' the articulation of his life's key principles. Joey O's caring instruction on the power of thought and goodness will change your life. Learning from Joey O has changed my life and the lives of so many wonderful people I know."

—Robert M. Kaminski, CEO, Leiner Health Products

"*Seeds of Wisdom* is an amazing, deeply touching book; one that I believe will improve the lives of everyone who reads it. It is wonderful to find an author who is so in touch with the world's gifts, and we are lucky he is generous enough to share his wisdom with us."

—Dave Hanson, Writer, *The Tonight Show with Jay Leno*

"In this book, from Groundwork to Harvest, Joey pays spiritual tribute to his beloved mother and to you, the reader . . . I'm honored to be one of his mentors and teachers, but most of all, his friend."

—Dr. Tom Costa, Clergyman

"We have never known a more radiantly positive person than you and greatly appreciate all that you do to enrich the lives of others."

—Stoney & Gloria DeMent, The Dyslexia Foundation

"Each generation is blessed with a writing that should not be missed. *Seeds of Wisdom* by Joey O is ours! A must-read about a beautiful relationship that will transcend eternity!"

—Stan Kahn, Vanguard Promotions & Marketing, Inc.

"You have a lot to give with the way you think about things. I enjoy and cherish your perspective and goodness. A lot of people can benefit from the seeds that you plant and share. You help remind me of the simple and powerful values of life . . ."

—Dr. Theresa Padilla, School of Metaphysics

"A tremendously beautiful story. Everyone should have a mother like Joey's and every mother should have a son like him."

—Charlie "Tremendous" Jones, President,
Life Management Services, Inc. and Executive Books

"Simply put and profound in content, *Seeds of Wisdom* is truly a must-read for any person aspiring to achieve an enhanced lifestyle and direction. This book offers guidelines and examples for success that can be applied by anyone at any time. Joey O has a true gift of synthesizing the complex into the simple. His own example of personal achievement takes it from fiction to reality. He is a one-of-a-kind athlete whose personal interest in others has led him to dedicate his life to helping others help themselves. Joey is a premiere example of how anyone can achieve—even beyond their dreams."

—Dr. James Melton, Speaker & Author,
and Dana Melton, Photographer

"Many people plant seeds and then trample on them with negative thinking. Joey O's book teaches you to focus on what you want, watering and fertilizing those seeds so that they will grow. Joey O has planted the right kind of seed and his tree has grown to have branches of encouragement, excellence, and enthusiasm. This book is the fruit of Joey's positive life."

—Allan D. Solheim, Executive Vice President,
Karsten Manufacturing Corporation

Praise for *The Dream Seed*

"Building dreams is a good profession—providing, of course, the architect has his feet on the ground. With his book, *The Dream Seed*, Joey O not only tells you how to dream, but how to make that dream become a reality. I consider Joey O a friend and a great entertainer. His positive attitude about life rubs off on you and makes you feel better. For children from ages 4 to 104, here is a truly inspiring story . . . a true story."

—Bob Hope

"It's too bad more kids don't grow up with the positive attitudes of Joey O. His book, *The Dream Seed*, is full of good philosophy for moving forward in life. We have already requested five copies to pass on to our granddaughters."

—President Gerald Ford & Mrs. Betty Ford

"As golf fans, we love Joey's act; but as parents and grandparents, we believe in and love his attitude in life."

—President George Bush & Mrs. Barbara Bush

"Joey, if *The Dream Seed* helps just one child, it will be worth all your effort."

—My Beloved Mom, Pat

ALSO BY JOEY O

The Dream Seed

To
Ron —
Best to you
Joey

SEEDS *of* WISDOM

SEEDS *of* WISDOM

A SON'S PROMISE KEPT

Joey O

EDITED BY TYLER BARRATT

A JOEY O PUBLICATION

AMERICA

Joey O is an acrobatic golf entertainer and author of the award-winning bestseller *The Dream Seed*. This is his second book.

FIRST EDITION

Published 2004. Printed in the United States of America

Editor Tyler Barratt
Contributing Editors Chelsea Samuelson and Carol Knight
Proofreader M. Lynette Austin

Cover Photo by Dana Melton
Book Design by Tyler Barratt

ISBN 0-9652234-1-8

This book is printed on acid-free paper.

1 3 5 7 9 10 8 6 4 2

In honor of my beloved mom,
and to the awesome invisibleness
that is in—and unites—all of us.

THE END.

The end of negative self-talk
The end of disharmonious thinking
The end of lack of action
The end of procrastination
The end of a defeatist attitude
The end of financial worry
The end of your body crying out for help
The end of using your intelligence unintelligently
The end of worrying about what others think about you
The end of keeping up with the Joneses
The end of a dull, uninspired, and uneventful life

It is time for a new beginning . . .

Yesterday ended last night and so can all of the above negations. So they will, if you make a decision right now to move forward with hope. I am honored to give this gift to you, and I ask that you finally take the responsibility needed to change your world. The following words will inspire and ignite that spark within. Your world is now excitement in action—so let's go turn your weeds into wisdom's seeds.

TABLE of CONTENTS

Acknowledgment . . . . *xv*

Letter to Mom . . . . *xvii*

Introduction . . . . *xix*

PART ONE | GROUNDWORK

1. Clearing & Preparing Your Mental Garden 3
2. Deciding to Decide 10
3. Fertilizer 13
4. The Growing Process 18
5. It's Your Garden 22

PART TWO | CULTIVATION

6. Friendliness, Happiness & Smiles. 29
7. The Gift Is in the Giving & the Gift Is in the Receiving. 34
8. Do You Own Your Possessions or Do They Own You?. 36
9. Remaining Youthful & Alive 38
10. Focus on the Good. 42
11. Peace & Health 44
12. Value You. 54
13. Everything Is a Gift If You Believe It Is. 57
14. The Dishwasher Lesson Can Work For You, Too 60
15. If You Can Dream It, You Can Do It 62

PART THREE | AFFIRMATION

16. What Is an Affirmation? 71
17. Daily Affirmations
    Finding the Right Relationship 75
    Keeping a Marriage Happy & Lasting 76
    Releasing a Material Object 77
    The Decision of Peace 78
    The Perfect Weight 79
    Energy 80
    Creative Imagination 81
    Being a Better Listener 82
    Integrity & Honesty 83
    Remaining Youthful Always 84
    Time & Timing 85
    Forgiving & Letting Go 86
    The Perfect Occupation 87
18. How to Write an Affirmation 88
19. Creating Your Affirmative Dream Seed Vision Book 90
20. Harvest Time 92

    Last Letter 95

ACKNOWLEDGMENT

Wow! Although taking credit for a life-inspiring book would be most flattering, I must give credit elsewhere. It seems that when I write, the pen in my hand just moves and wonderful ideas flow through me so perfectly, so effortlessly, and so inspirationally. I feel it is a calling and that I am just an instrument to unite and connect that invisibleness in each of us.

In the words of *Seeds of Wisdom,* I felt as though that wonderful invisibleness that connected my mom and me will always be there. It was like my mom was sitting right next to me—guiding, directing, sharing, inspiring, and giving me the memories and gifts of lessons from over forty years ago to the present moments. The connection is so real, and I am so grateful knowing we are still one in CONSCIOUSNESS. Twenty-four years ago, when I was brushing my teeth, I looked into the mirror and thought, "Someone's gonna make the world laugh—it might as well be me." The inspiration and idea of giving happiness to people by being an acrobatic golf entertainer had just dawned on me. Now all of these wonderful years later, the title, which I knew would come to me at the perfect time and place, actually did—*Seeds of Wisdom.* I truly believe that just as I bring happiness to people through performing, the words that you are about to read will bring happiness to your life. They are gifts from my mom and her goodness, which

inspired that invisibleness in me so we could share these words that will lead you to examine your invisible thoughts, mental pictures, verbal words, and then realize how this is an amazing mirror image of your life. My first book, *The Dream Seed*, took nearly two-and-a-half years to complete only thirty-two pages. Writing *Seeds of Wisdom* took a fraction of the time, as the awesome ideas and memories flowed easily. I was DIVINELY GUIDED to help people learn from my mom's example and her beautiful attitude towards life.

So I now acknowledge that invisible thing that we all possess and all have in common. May these wonderful ideas and thoughts, which my mom shared with me, now be the ultimate gift to you. Life really is a series of invisible things that are planted, nurtured, fertilized, and cultivated. It is we who live our lives, and it is we who can use this gift for lack or abundance, harmony or disharmony, love or hate. May this gift be so self-examining that you make a decision today and forevermore to use your gift of life in a way that brings GOODNESS to the invisibleness in you and to everyone you come in contact with.

I wish you only GOODNESS, and may *Seeds of Wisdom* be your ultimate gift.

Joey O

NOVEMBER 15, 2002

This is the letter that I wrote to my mom before she went into the hospital for surgery. She said it was beautiful and should be published; little did I know at the time that it would be . . .

Dear Mom,

Usually writing letters comes very easy, yet this time just getting started has taken much longer; but finally the pen is moving, and I hope I can express my feelings and gratitude in the way I truly feel from my heart. When someone gives you the gift of life and you see that person handling a challenge with the strength that you are, one realizes that a parent really is always teaching their child about life and sharing their love in a multitude of ways. I appreciate and admire your attitude and courage so much— although being a beginner in this thing called life—when I recall past challenging situations of friends and relatives. I realize your handling the process of overcoming this challenge has truly been monumental and one of a kind. This has shown me so much about the strength of your mind and the GOODNESS of your soul. Had God allowed me the option to go through the process so you would not have to, I would have gladly accepted it just to be able to see you in perfect health. But knowing how much we both think alike, I know that the situation would have been tougher on you than this is, that is why you can feel how much I feel for you. I haven't handled this with nearly the strength you have. I have so much faith that you are DIVINELY GUIDED and that all will go perfectly. It is seeing you go through the process that hurts, because I just want you to be yourself and do your usual daily fun things without having to go through this. Just like a parent doesn't want to see a child go through challenges, and I can only speak for me, the last thing I ever would want to see is you going through this process. Reclaiming your perfect health with your will and attitude will be achieved better and faster than anyone I know. Just know that even while you're in Maryland, I'll be there, too, and I know the truth about you. Please just have that knowingness (no matter what the opinions of anyone are) that you know the truth about you and that unexplainable situations appear and unexplainable situations disappear. Healing happens daily, and with a belief of knowing the truth, you too will experience a healing and know I'll be here when you return and will help you get through this healing process. Just know and picture God in your liver—God is perfect and so are you—just believe this along with me and all those who are praying. Know I love you with every fiber of my being, and I am with you in CONSCIOUSNESS now and for always.

I love you, Mom.

Joey

INTRODUCTION

This book came about in March of 2003, when my beloved mom was in her final days at the National Institute of Health in Bethesda, Maryland. During this time, I promised my mom that I would write another book, based on what she taught me, to help humanity move forward. The words in this book are from the lessons my mom taught me over the past forty-five years, even up to her final moments, and from the application of these lessons to my life. I continue to learn and grow from my mother's wisdom and perfect attitude towards life.

The wisdom in this book is most simple, and you will discover your true self quickly, easily, and effortlessly. You'll learn why you have not manifested some wonderful things in your world, and you will learn to put into practice some fast and easy ways to make sure you plant and grow only successful dream seeds. It does work every time and will totally change the way you think and talk about yourself and your wishes, as well as change the way you manifest beautiful and awesome successes in your world. Through the proper self-talk, self-visualizing, and easy actions, you'll learn to use your intelligence intelligently. You will be able to release the "weeds" in your mental garden and focus on what you truly want in life. Every time your life seems to be a mess, you are there—just because you go through darkness does not mean you have to stop and build a house there. Through learning the law of cause and effect and using it intelligently, you will demonstrate the truth about you, and this truth will set you free. This is not a momentary truth; it is a lifetime truth. You will learn to know and love my mom, and she'll be a huge inspiration to you—her attitude, wisdom, and courage will truly spark you, leaving you feeling as though you knew her well. Our CREATOR makes only GOODNESS. What does that leave out? Absolutely nothing—you included. You are a valuable, worthwhile person, and it is high time you realize the abundance, happiness, and perfect health that are your birthrights; claim them now and forevermore.

You will learn to know that we are always creating something in our world, and the real question will be, *what are you thinking about?* You will realize that we might as well think of abundance and goodness because our mind does not care what we focus on, but it will grow whatever we focus on. So be careful what you dwell on.

Let's get going on these fun and simple ways to release negativity, the concern of what others think of us, the need to be right, and the ego and its chatter. You will focus on planting and growing peace, happiness, abundance, and self-discovery in simple, practical fundamentals. I am grateful that you have allowed my mom in your world—a new world for you—a world of changing thoughts, words, and actions, all for your highest good. This change in your life is an awesome way to manifest only GOOD.

So let's go, it is great fun, and know from this moment on that you are planting and growing wonderful dream seeds that are perfect, whole, and complete. The good news is you have little to learn—a beautiful life is more about subtraction than addition. You'll subtract all the weeds that have kept your garden from growing abundantly and add only GOODNESS to your world. Once again, it's time to use your intelligence intelligently, and we (my mom and I) believe that by the end of this book you will know this truth, and it will be your responsibility (to respond with ability) to put it into action. Let's go together on this wonderful journey . . .

PART ONE | GROUNDWORK

CHAPTER ONE

Clearing & Preparing Your Mental Garden

Every child should be as lucky as me,
to have such a wonderful mom like mine. Wow.

"I'm not going to think about it," my mom said as I asked her about her health challenge. My mom had the most incredible use of mind I have ever witnessed. She was teaching me the law of cause and effect at that very moment, as she had been for years. She was teaching me that our minds don't care what we plant in them any more than the soil in the ground cares what we plant in it. Carrot seeds always grow into carrots—no exceptions. It's the law. It is impossible to plant carrot seeds and grow cucumbers. Why? Because there is intelligence within a carrot seed to know that it can and must grow beautiful orange carrots. Likewise, our mental garden does not care what we plant in it. I had an aunt who always spoke of illness and disharmony. Guess what—she lived a lonely, disharmonious, unhealthy life. The law of cause and effect says what we plant, we get—either in our mental garden or in the physical soil.

My mom always spoke of the good. When she lost her left eye to ocular melanoma, one would have thought she had only scraped her finger. In fact, I've heard more people complain about scraping their finger than my mom ever did about her eye. She would say that many people are far worse off than she, and she remained focused on her good eye. I remember her saying that she would help others going through this unusual challenge, and she did. You see, my mom taught me, "We don't always get in life what we want—but we always get what we think about and take action on." What we think about expands. We are given free will—the ability to decide what we want to plant in our mental garden. As you observe and listen to others, pay careful attention to the words they choose. Before long you can predict their level of abundance, health, happiness, and success.

One reason some people do not move forward in life is because they use their past as a calling card. These people believe that just because something negative happened to them in the past, they have to dwell on it—as if wearing it as a badge or medal around their necks. This constant talk of yesterday does not serve them, and actually blocks them from their good in the present moment. Pull these weeds and focus on what you want. The negative past doesn't serve you now—get over it and do not think about it, do not talk about it, do not explain it. Focus on what you want, not what you do not want.

The thoughts we think determine whether we swim or sink, and the words we choose determine whether we win or lose. So, if what we talk about and what we think about grows—from our invisible worlds to our physical worlds—it is vital to think and use words in an affirmative way—which will bring GOODNESS to us and also to others. When our self-talk and thoughts are awesome, we will take action on them.

Action is the name of the game—use it properly and life will never be the same.

So this brings us to knowing the truth—the truth that will set us free for always, in all ways. When our thinking is negative, our lives will be disharmonious, and we will still get exactly what we planted in our mental gardens—the mind doesn't care if it's good or not so good.

Before we plant a beautiful garden, we must clear and prepare the soil. We must remove the garbage, the weeds, and the unneeded "stuff" that will get in the way of the beautiful growth. Before we can grow and live a beautiful, harmonious life, we must also remove all doubt, all fear, all discord, all past negativity, all the mental weeds to clear the path and prepare our minds to have the clear, clean open space and attitude for abundant growth. So you can see, as I mentioned earlier, that growing a wonderful life is more about subtraction than addition. When we are born, we are like a clear, beautiful, and perfect diamond. As time goes on, we hear and see negative things. It is like coal piling up on our diamond. Sometimes a well-meaning adult or friend may say something negative about us or our dreams, and even more coal—more doubt, more fear—pile up. As time passes, we can no longer see the beautiful diamond. It is covered up, yet the diamond is still there. So it is our goal to do our mental and verbal activities to remove the coal and allow the diamond to shine through once again. In essence, we want to become as intelligent as the day we were born—without fear, doubt, judgment, negativity, disharmony, and lack of self-esteem. These are all learned behaviors that can be unlearned, and the time to start is now.

Just as an ice sculptor makes beautiful designs and figures by removing unneeded ice to create his masterpiece, we also can recreate our positive mental attitude. Our mental weeds keep us from true happiness, and it is high time that people spend as much time removing these mental weeds as they do in removing the actual weeds in their backyard gardens.

We don't need to get anything; we have all we need, and just by doing the activities in this chapter, we can cultivate an awesome attitude like my mom had. As they wheeled my mom into experimental surgery in November 2002, she said, "If things don't go well, it's been a lot of fun." Wow, what an attitude of gratitude for life.

We, too, must be grateful for our time here and the ability to grow, learn, demonstrate, and share our GOODNESS. It is darkest before dawn. Let us know this now, and plant what we want and turn away from what we don't want. Let yesterday end last night and let us move forward, releasing the past and planting a new future. Now!

There is a story of two Buddhist monks who are preparing to cross over a large stream of water. A town beggar, a real troublemaker, came pleading for them to help him across. The first monk said, "No, you are mean to all." The second monk obliged, saying, "Yes, I'll help you across." Fifteen minutes later, the monk who didn't help the beggar across said to the other, "I can't believe you helped that no-good so-and-so across." The other monk replied, "I dropped him off fifteen minutes ago—why are you still carrying him with you?"

As my mom said, "I'm not going to think about it." Let go of your past challenges—let go of all anger, doubt, and fear—pull those weeds up by affirming what you do want, and watch your world grow beautifully. Always remember that the law is impersonal—our minds will grow whatever we focus on and nurture. The mind does not care what it is nurturing. We have free will, so it is up to us to plant something beautiful and share it with others. My mom had a beautiful way of avoiding a conflict. She would simply change the subject to something more harmonious—she was teaching me to release negativity and plant affirmations and good. We can do this by following these affirmations and actions:

AFFIRM OUT LOUD DAILY

- Today and forevermore I release all disharmonious and negative thoughts. I let them go now.
- Yesterday ended last night. I think about the good.
- I tune out and let go of all disharmonious people, places, and things. I accept only wonderful, loving people and situations in my world.
- I know anger may lead to danger. I think of peace and GOODNESS and accept it in my world now.

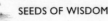

THINGS TO DO

- Do not read any negative articles in newspapers or magazines.
- Do not watch any negative television programs, especially the news. Limit your time spent watching television.
- Do not listen to negative and depressing music.
- Think happy and uplifting thoughts and picture them in your mind.
- It is often wiser to unlearn than to learn—focus on releasing past negative attitudes and episodes, and focus on planting your new wonderful dream seeds.
- Walk through nature for a minimum of 30 minutes daily for 30 days (and you'll do it the rest of your life).
- Speak words that affirm success, perfect health, abundance, love, riches, happiness, and joy.
- Always speak kindly to yourself and about yourself. Never belittle yourself.
- Find humor in yourself and others—life is too important to be taken seriously. None of us is going to get out of here alive.
- Laugh out loud daily.
- Look for good in others and compliment them on this good.

THINGS TO DO (continued)

- Invest your time with fun, optimistic, and fun-loving people.
- Catch and watch your words and thoughts daily. Always word things in the affirmative; never use a negative word in a positive affirmation.
- Read uplifting material that is motivational and inspirational.

So we must be reminded of what we once forgot—to be as smart as the day we were born. Release the past negativity that has accumulated by speaking, thinking, and acting on unwanted desires. We must put our attention on the GOOD by releasing all doubt, all fear, and all discord, as we prepare our mental garden to grow and demonstrate GOODNESS. Remember, it takes self-responsibility not to react, talk, and think about how and what we responded to in the past—it no longer serves us. Remove those mental weeds and plant hope, faith, happiness, and abundance—it's great fun and it works. Do these releasing activities daily and then plant new seeds—it is up to you. Our CREATOR doesn't move parked cars. Action, action, action—did I say action?

CHAPTER TWO

Deciding to Decide

What you focus on, you become.

My mom put her attention on life and living. She was always conscious of focusing on enjoying her days and sharing her smile and goodness with her friends. My amazing mom chose to mentally turn away from challenges, and instead she focused on the solutions.

In the last chapter, we discussed negation in our mental garden and the preparation of our minds to plant what we truly desire. Now it is time to write down and list what you want. Please be definite and take as much time as needed. Of course we all want abundance, health, happiness, friends, and so on. List them. How much abundance? (Be specific.) Where would you like to be monetarily in one year? How about in five years? What kind of health do you desire? Perfect, of course. We must be grateful for perfect health while we have it and claim more for ourselves continuously. What kind of friends? How many? What kind of goals? Do you want a new occupation? What type of occupation? (Again, be specific.) Do you need a better home or a new car? It can be invisible or material. Please take this time and list what you truly want; no thought should be paid to what you don't want. Write down only what you desire. Please add a time frame to the list that dictates when you would like to achieve your dream seed. Nature's law may have a different time frame in mind—so be patient—remember in every delay something better is on the way. Since we manifest in our physical worlds what we dwell upon in our mental worlds, it is absolutely crucial to put your attention and intention on what you want and pay no attention to what you do not want. Don't ever verbalize what you do not want. Even not making a decision is a decision. Not caring for your garden produces weeds, and not planting goodness in your mind will develop mental weeds. Don't do this to yourself—plant only abundance and GOODNESS. You will grow whatever you focus on, so you might as well plant something awesome and share it. Use your intelligence intelligently! The law of growth is impersonal—it doesn't care who succeeds and who fails. So let us put into action what we want and realize we are always planting something and growing what we dwell on.

Picture in your mind the perfect end result of your dream seed and be conscious of it daily. See it, feel it, smell it, and know it. Know what brings GOODNESS to you will also help you bring GOODNESS to humanity.

As the saying goes, *People don't plan to fail; they just fail to plan.* Decide what you desire; believe it and know it. Many people spend more time planning a vacation than they do their own lives. Remember, we all live the life we imagine. The real question is, *what are we imagining?* Please know everything is created twice—first by that invisible thing called thought (a decision), and then by taking action and growing it into our physical worlds. From the invisible to the visible . . .

Decide upon what you desire and know that an acorn seed, after only one day of growth, is still an oak tree—tiny as it may be. Your dream seed is growing, and as small as it is, it is still present, so allow it to grow in nature's time. Do not rush its growth, yet fertilize it daily with verbal affirmations, mentally focusing on it and picturing it perfectly. Believe and have FAITH. With fertilization, your dream seed will grow.

AFFIRM OUT LOUD DAILY

- I may not know what is best for me at this time, but something inside me does, and it reveals itself to me at the perfect time and place.
- I gratefully accept perfect health in my world. It is planted perfectly and grows even more perfectly within me.
- I plant the perfect thoughts in my mind and put the perfect foods in my body.
- I am a grand friend and share my friendship.
- I have perfect happiness, and I share my happiness.

CHAPTER THREE

Fertilizer

When you value the invisible, you get the visible.

I remember my mom sharing many other wonderful sayings with me—

"Make hay while the sun shines."

"Live and let live."

"Never wish your life away."

"Be on time."

"Don't compare yourself with others—be the best you can be."

"If your book, *The Dream Seed*, helps only one person, it's well worth your effort."

All these are wonderful ideas and fertilizer for your decision. Let me elaborate. We need to water our dream seeds daily and pay careful attention to them. There are three invisible fertilizers that, when used properly, can make our invisible thoughts visible. The first is to make perfect use of our time. The second is to utilize our minds' creative imaginations. Third, of course, is our belief and faith in our dreams. When we value the invisible (time, mind, belief), we get the visible.

Let's begin with the first fertilizer—time. We all get the same twenty-four hours in one day. I don't get twenty-seven, and you don't get twelve. We all get the same. It is how well you budget and use your time that will really demonstrate how perfectly you accomplish your dream seeds. I remember practicing fourteen hours a day while working at midnight for the *Iowa City Press Citizen*, stuffing flyer ads in the local newspaper. I practiced during the daylight and worked at night. I had two goals daily—to make perfect use of my time and to be better than I was the day prior. Minute by minute, hour by hour, day by day, week by week, month by month, and year by year, it had a truly compounding effect on perfecting my skills. Mom said, "Make hay while the sun shines," and I do. Mom said, "Never wish your life away" (be in the moment—enjoy and be productive in the now), and I do. Make each day count even if you're bad at math. (This not only makes sense in the long run, but many dollars.) Take control of your time now and you'll have control of your life in the future. Now when people say, "I'd give my life to hit a golf ball like you, Joey O," I reply, "I did." I know that the only person who controlled my destiny was looking at me in the mirror daily. I know that the ten most important two-letter words in the world are: *if it is to be, it is up to me.*

It all goes back to that invisible thing called time. You can't see it, but you can see the results of using it marvelously and to perfection. Wisdom is knowledge in action. Get into action and practice your affirmations, visualize your dream seeds as if they are already grown to perfection. Budget your time to perfection. Remember, our FAITH doesn't move parked cars. Take action and control of your time and move forward through that awesome fertilizer called time.

The second amazing fertilizer is your mind—your creative imagination. You can't see the mind at work—it is invisible. But you can see what happens when you use your creative intelligence intelligently. When my mom taught me not to compare myself to others, she was teaching me to be me. She taught me to not be afraid to be different, and that it's okay not to conform. I learned that I didn't need to be like others and belong to a group; I could be a fringe dweller and be out there on my own. Mom also said to me frequently, "Live and let live." Live your life and allow the world and others to be who they are—they have their own expressions of belief.

While working at the *Iowa City Press Citizen*, I put my mind not on the task at hand (stuffing ads in the paper for minimum wage), but on my show, which was my dream seed. I pictured myself in front of people, getting them to laugh and smile, by thinking up new creative golf shots. I just used my imagination and time intelligently, not focusing on the boredom at work, but on the excitement and creativity I could show in the future.

Being different is great fun for me, and it can be for you as well. I remember when I was learning to hit a golf ball while on top of a six-foot unicycle. Not only did I miss the ball, but I also had a hard time riding the darn unicycle. But in my mind I could do it, and do it perfectly.

Never see things as they are; you should see things as you want them to be. See your dream seed perfectly complete in your mind's eye and let it grow (it has to; it is the law of the mind and the law of cause and effect in action). Being different and focused on coming up with imaginative ideas is so rewarding. When you train your mind, awesome ideas come to you at the perfect time and place. Word of guidance . . . have a pencil and paper handy at all times so you can jot down the awesome ideas, which will come to you, and remember to take action on them. So, as you can see, fertilizer number two is the mind. It is vital. Know that it will bring GOODNESS to you, and even more importantly, to humanity. Share your creativity.

The third fertilizer is belief and faith. They, too, are invisible; yet used properly, they will bring your dream seed to the physical. The secret is to believe in yourself when no one else will. Never accept *no* for an answer, unless *no* is the answer you want. Know that when others say *no*, it is temporary. Just keep moving forward.

I remember that my mom was so proud of me for keeping my faith of entertaining on The Tonight Show. It took me twenty-seven years for that dream seed to grow, but it did grow awesomely. I even drove from Iowa to California, snuck into the producer's office, and told him that I dreamt every day since I was a little boy of making his audience smile. He basically gave me no hope, but I did not believe a word he said. I just kept practicing every day—all day—visualizing that audience smiling. I took action, I wrote, and I called. They kept turning me down, and I just kept believing and taking action. After believing every day and taking action every day for twenty-seven years, on December 22, 1997, I was on The Tonight Show with Jay Leno, along with Tiger Woods.

My dream seed grew from an invisible thought that I had when I was a little boy growing up without a television set, not even knowing what I would do to make the audience smile, to a reality. I knew Johnny Carson was born in Avoka, Iowa, and if he could make millions laugh, then I could at least make people smile. I knew that the law had to grow this dream seed. I planted it, I nurtured it, and I believed in it. You can, too. In fact, you are—as we speak—because you now have no excuse; you now know the law of cause and effect and how it works, and with your newfound self-responsibility, you know: *if it is to be, it is up to me.* Believe in yourself even when no one else does. To be successful, it is best not to play follow the follower. Know what you want, be different, and go for it. What others think of us is of no importance, as long as we do not harm anyone, and especially if we are bringing GOODNESS to humanity and ourselves.

Being honest to oneself is the key fertilizer. Making the best use of your time is in essence being honest to yourself, because this way you can reach your dreams. By using your creative imagination while being honest to yourself, you can grow abundantly. Honesty is being the best you can be each day. This is important if you are to grow to your fullest. And if not, get out the weed digger because you'll have to waste time and energy on the weeds. It is much easier to plant GOODNESS and honesty, and if you do, you won't have to waste that important time and creativity undoing what you could have done correctly the first time. It's your choice.

CHAPTER FOUR

The Growing Process

We don't always get what we want in life,
but we always get what we think about and take action on.

My mom's all-time favorite quote was, "It's only a hobby." I think of it and use it all the time. It has especially sunk in tremendously since her transition from this world. My mom knew that the real secret to abundant living was about enjoying and sharing the moment, and knowing that life was too important to be taken seriously. My mom knew the secret was to have fun every day and share her smile and good nature with others. She dressed so tastefully, yet her finest accessory was her beautiful smile. She smiled with her whole being—everyone loved "Patty." Mom knew the gift was in the giving, sharing herself and her wonderful way and attitude with all her friends. She would even purposefully lose at card games to see her friends smile. She used to tell me, "Do your thing." She knew that I would only be happiest when I lived my life the way I wanted to and shared my smile and talent with others the way I chose to. Others thought I was crazy (it does help to be a little crazy in the entertainment business) to think I could make a living hitting golf balls in entertaining ways. I remember when I first started out, and no one would have me perform, not even for free. I was getting kind of skinny from training so much and Mom snuck me a twenty dollar bill for food, saying with her smile, "Don't tell anyone." Mom taught me to be careful of what I said, too. She would tell me, "Don't bite the hand that feeds you." I still remember her wonderful ways and can hear her voice often. I am feeling and hearing it right now. Knowing as my mom did, "It's only a hobby," we need not dwell on what happens to us. We need to focus on reacting to it harmoniously.

A missed golf shot is just a missed golf shot—"It's only a hobby." My mentor and best friend, Bob Vavra, taught me to react to situations with this question: Will this incident affect me one hour from now, one day from now, one week from now, one month from now, or one year from now? If it will affect you in the long run, it is something to focus on. If not, let it go—right now.

Enjoy the growth of your dream seed—the most fun time for me was being so excited about the possibilities of the learning process and growing each day. Sometimes months will go by and that little acorn seed won't show signs of growth. Things happen to it; it gets covered with snow, even a dog may come by and water it. But remember the law of cause and effect: what you plant, you get. The acorn has to grow into an oak tree and over time it does; giving us beautiful shade, a home to squirrels, leaves to help build dwellings for animals, more seeds for more beautiful trees to grow, food for animals, and on and on it goes. Remember, one kernel of corn produces one stalk, from that one stalk comes a row the next year, from that comes one acre the next, and from one acre comes a whole farm of hundreds of acres. One little thought will manifest into a beautiful life through affirmative self-talk, visualization of what you want, perfect use of your mind, time and beliefs; most importantly, this will happen by listening to the beautiful and beloved role models (like my mom), and by taking action on their words and never letting them leave your CONSCIOUSNESS—never, never, never.

CHAPTER FIVE

It's Your Garden

The only person who can control your destiny
is looking right at you in the mirror.

It is your garden, your world, your CONSCIOUSNESS, and your decision of what to plant and what to allow in your life.

I have been told we do not see the world as it is—we see it as we think it is. If you talk to someone who reads the newspaper daily, and who continuously watches and listens to the news on television and radio, their perception of the world is far different from someone who instead prefers to walk through the woods investing their time and mind positively, rather than in a world of negativity. It all comes down to the choice of what you allow into your CONSCIOUSNESS. So you see, we are not what we think we are—yet what we think, we are. Ask yourself—what am I doing with my time, and what am I allowing in my mental garden? The constant, day-by-day bombardment of negativity into your world has a long-term detrimental effect on your subconscious. It makes your perception of the world far worse than it really is. You can choose that world if you want, but why? There are thousands of people who are giving to charities, raising awareness for something good. There are books, magazines, tapes, and even some good TV shows that can add knowledge and wisdom to educate your mental garden. Be very careful what you allow in, and be careful not to allow negative people in your world. Remember, it is you that allows this negativity in, and it is time you allowed it to go. Unless, that is, you enjoy it. But do you really?

As a young boy I was frequently confused because I treated everyone with GOODNESS, kindness, and respect—yet, unfortunately, I wasn't always treated this way in return. I spoke to my mom about this. My mom replied, "Joey, you can not expect others to be like you. You just keep being the best person that you can be. That is what is important." This is truly one of the most valuable lessons that I could have ever learned. My mom was teaching me to be kind, even in the face of disharmony and discord. No matter what was happening in my outside world, I could choose peace and self-love on the inside. Mom was teaching me that others' opinions of me were none of my business. All I could control was myself and not let their attitude dictate and control how I felt about myself. I knew that I was, and am, a GOOD soul and a GOOD person—no matter what others said.

I remember my grandma, my mom's mom, who never once said a negative statement about anyone. She was beautiful on the inside and outside, just as my mother was. I have also obtained some wonderful advice from my father. He taught me to "zip it." This simple saying means so much. My father is the most honest man that I have ever met, and he has always told me to "zip it" when it comes to trying to solve situations with my lips. It is true that sometimes one must stand up for oneself, but arguments are often unproductive—so avoid them at any and all costs. As the saying goes, "A man or woman convinced against his or her will is of the same opinion still." So just be the best that you can be, and do not spend your precious time convincing others of your opinion or worrying about their opinions. Each of us is entitled to our own opinions, which is what makes us so special and unique.

It is your garden. Plant optimism, plant abundance, plant hope, and most of all, take responsibility for not allowing the weeds to enter your garden. You'll have enough challenges (lessons) along the way without clouding your mental health with mental weeds. Release the type of soil that makes it easy for those weeds to manifest.

AFFIRM OUT LOUD DAILY

- I allow good news, exciting news, and productive news in my world. Thank you.
- Carefully, I examine what to allow in my world. I know what to do and do it perfectly. Thank you.
- No longer do the television, newspaper, radio, food, or negative people own me; I have total control over what I allow in my mind and body. Effortlessly, I allow only that which is good. Thank you.
- I focus on the good and the good grows perfectly. Thank you.

PART TWO | CULTIVATION

CHAPTER SIX

Friendliness, Happiness & Smiles

*Focus on what you can bring to
a relationship, not what you can get from it.*

Everyone loved my mom. Her attitude and smile were so beautiful. She was the light in a dark room. I am honored when people say that I, too, possess that quality. I received that gift from my mom. She would tell me, "Be who you are and allow others to be who they are." My mom, by example, taught me to smile so very much. She was a smiler and loved to have fun. (That's probably how I became the class clown.) As I have mentioned before, my mom dressed so tastefully, yet her finest and most memorable accessory was her cheery smile. My attitude was never to let success go to my clothes, yet like my mom, I always smiled and waved to people. In fact, one of my most awesome experiences was when I wintered in California. I got a condo out there, in fact the first home I ever purchased, and when I would go get my mail, walk, or bike in the complex, I'd be smiling and waving to people, and they would totally ignore me. I then knew that this wasn't Mayberry, so I planted a dream seed just to be my friendly self. This was their consciousness, not mine, and I wasn't about to change and own their way of life. So I just kept on smiling and waving. I was friendly to all, and by the time I sold that place three years later, people were stopping their cars on the street and coming out of their homes to talk to me. In fact, one day six cars stopped and blocked traffic while people came out to say howdy to me. So like my mom, I learned that to have a friend, first be a friend. In other words—if you don't have friends, work on your friendliness. Happiness is truly unique. Unlike most things, the more happiness you give, the more you get in return. My folks taught me early on that I wasn't more important than the next person, and they were not more important than me. We are all equal. "You can tell a person by the books they read and the friends they keep," Dr. James and Dana Melton, two wonderful friends of mine, once told me. Dr. Melton is a wonderful writer and speaker. I highly suggest reading his books or hearing him speak. His wife, Dana, is one of the most talented photographers I have ever seen—you should check out her work (e.g., the photograph on the cover of this book). I like to say *the friends you keep can make you smile or weep*. So it is important to be friendly to all.

I heard it takes forty-seven muscles to frown and only a lucky thirteen to smile—that shows it is easier to share a smile with others than to frown all by your lonesome. There is no single way to happiness; happiness is the single way. If you're looking for your happiness in others, you'll look for a lifetime. Happiness is something to give to others, not get. By the sheer act of giving happiness, you'll receive more than you ever dreamt of. Happiness cannot be bought, but it can be taught. So focus on giving your smile away—you have no shortage of those thirteen muscles.

Mom would allow others to win. She kept her peace, and actually both parties won in the long run. She knew life wasn't always about winning or losing. It was about having fun in the moment and allowing the people you were sharing your time with to enjoy the moment. She took responsibility to do her part so that others would smile, too.

I remember my mom also saying to me, "Birds of a feather flock together . . . The apple doesn't fall far from the tree . . . Can't change the spots on a leopard." All of these sayings are interrelated, and I believe my mom was telling me several things. For one, many people do not like change; they want to hang around people that they are familiar with and remain in their chosen environment. (Have you been to your high school reunion lately?) My mom was also teaching me that to be successful in life, I needed to be friends with all different types of people, and I am. I have friends who are very poor financially, but we get along great because we have happy attitudes. I also have friends who have more money than they could spend in one hundred lifetimes, and we get along great because we have happy attitudes. One great lesson I've learned from this is that one's financial wealth has nothing to do with his happiness. People may live more abundantly with more money, but that doesn't guarantee more smiles. In fact, it has been my experience that unless people choose to change their spots (attitudes), they won't grow. I've been told I never met a stranger. I guess I've always been one to smile, wave, and say "hi" first. It's fun for me, and it cheers people up.

We should expand our CONSCIOUSNESS to learn to get along with new people—grow, explore, experience all types of new friends. If we keep doing the same ol' things the same ol' way, we live the same ol' life

with the same ol' strife. Many people are using their energy in such an unintelligent way. Many are afraid to let loose, to let their friends see them having fun, and to be childlike for even an hour. Start laughing more, living more, and quit worrying about what others think of you. Remember my mom's saying, "It's only a hobby." Have fun, share your fun, and live your fun! Give the richness of your GOODNESS and smiles, and then watch your garden grow abundantly without the worry, fear, and discord of others' thoughts. It is your life and it is meant for living. Now!

AFFIRM OUT LOUD DAILY

- I always meet new wonderful people and share many laughs with them.
- My life is exciting, and I share my smile with new, wonderful people.
- I say hello first, I wave first, and I smile first.
- My world is safe, and I am always guided to safe places.
- I grow and explore new places, new people, and new environments—all are safe and fun.

CHAPTER SEVEN

The Gift Is in the Giving
& the Gift Is in the Receiving

Find your gift and give it.

One day my mom was wearing some pretty earrings, and her friend Helen, from Iowa, commented to my mom on how much she liked them. My mom immediately removed them from her ears and gave them to Helen. That was so much like my mom. Her friend Jan, who has a wonderful sense of humor like my mom's, said, "Gosh, I hope no one comments on your undergarments!" My mom was so thoughtful, and she was never attached to a material object. She taught me—by example—never to let a material object own me, and I live by that today. My mom never forgot a birthday, holiday, or special occasion. To this day, I have every letter and card she ever gave me, and they mean more to me than any material possession ever has. The real gift for my mom was to see the joy in others, and she did her best to add her personal touch to life. I so often remember my mom getting invited to dinner at someone's home. She would immediately respond, "Oh, don't go to the trouble, we'll take you out to eat." My mom didn't want to put anyone out. Afterwards, my mom would tell me about these situations, and I suggested allowing others to do little nice things like having her over for dinner. Being a wonderful receiver is, in essence, a gift to the other person. Like my mom, I've learned to be a wonderful giver, and that I also need to be a better receiver. If someone would make a kind comment on my shirt, book, or whatever, I would give it as a gift to the person. Like my mom, I also get a bigger smile giving it away than from owning it. I believe it is necessary to learn to just say, "Thank you, that's kind of you, I accept your generosity." You are really allowing them the gift of giving, just like they would enjoy the gifts we give. My mom was always thinking of others. She would make soup if someone was ill, send flowers, and give special gifts. Never have I seen a more thoughtful, giving person and a more beautiful role model for all of us.

I have come to realize why I am always calm and relaxed when I perform and speak in front of large groups; I am focused on giving and sharing happiness and inspiration. My attention is on the audience, not on me, and when your attention is not on yourself, it is impossible to get nervous. This is common sense. So give, share, and show your gratitude. As a result, your life will become more exciting, fun, and peaceful.

CHAPTER EIGHT

Do You Own Your Possessions or Do They Own You?

Life is a ride, not a race.

I frequently wonder how many decisions people make throughout each day, and each life, based on what others will think of them. "Oh," they may think, "I can't drive this type of car, people will think less of me . . . I can't live in this neighborhood, people won't think highly of me . . . I can't wear this type of clothing, people won't think I'm successful . . ." On and on it goes. People who are not even financially able to play this dreadful game still play it; what others think of them seems to be more important than what they think of themselves. They live a terribly frustrated and disharmonious life in an endless downward spiral because they are allowing others to control their world. Living below your means will not only give you more control of your financial world, but it will also give you more peace, happiness, and freedom. It's time for you to get control of what is best for you and your family—not the approval of your neighbors, friends, family, relatives, and television commercials. Seeking approval is a disapproving act. It is your life, not theirs, and it is time to live in your world. Ironically, neighbors pay little attention to you and are more worried about keeping up with the other neighbors. People are creating dis-ease in their worlds in playing this game. Never—ever—let a material object own you. Never allow what others think of you control you. Never get a bigger house just to store stuff you don't even use.

If you want to recognize your peace again, value your own ideas. Do not worry about what others think. If you play this self-defeating game, it is time to start anew. If you don't play it, way to go—and don't ever get sucked into it. It cannot help you, and it surely will not help others.

CHAPTER NINE

Remaining Youthful & Alive

You don't know how you will die, but you can choose how to live.

You don't have to let an old person move into your CONSCIOUSNESS. So often when I am with people, I hear them affirm their illnesses and challenges. This is especially true with seniors—they think because of their age it is okay to accept and talk about illness and challenges. Well the doctors may say that they have—let's say, arthritis—but every time they think of that word, say that word, or affirm that condition, they are fertilizing more abundant arthritis. They are using their intelligence unintelligently. They are allowing an old person to move in, without even realizing it. Is this what they want? Life is to be lived, so why allow it to be lived disharmoniously, full of pain, and full of illness? Put your attention on what you want—health and freedom of movement. Imagine the results that would occur if for every time someone affirmed the negativity of an illness or a challenge, they would instead affirm perfect health? Their lives would be so much happier and full of peace. Watch the way you self-talk on this topic. Always think health, affirm health, and talk yourself into perfect health. The way you think and talk to yourself is a mirror image of the demonstration of your life and how you live it daily. Correct your self-talk now, and each and every time you are tempted to get sympathy from others, stop and realize you are only adding more negativity into your world. Think weed-eater and turn it around. My friend and teacher, Dr. Tom Costa, teaches this attitude to perfection. He is a perfect example of walking his talk. If you get to Palm Desert, California, give yourself a gift and listen to his words. (He is truly a gift to the world and has taught me so much.) Say the opposite of the condition and claim youth and perfect health now and for always, in all ways—it's so much easier, so much more intelligent, and so much healthier for you.

Never use words like pain, hurt, etc.—these are the words of an illness. I'll never even wear a shirt or hat if a word on it reflects an illness or disease. I don't even want to see the word in print, or even hear the word on TV or radio, or get into discussions pertaining to the words of dis-ease. Would you rather experience the beauty in the garden of life or the ugliness of a weed-filled existence? It is your choice. The best time to talk about illness is to your doctor.

So please use your intelligence intelligently and kick that old person and old attitude out! Allow that young, excited, and healthy person to come on out and play once again. People will show you abundant admiration for your new attitude. You will attract positive people in your "new world." This negative self-talk is learned, and this behavior can and must be unlearned now. It is not healthy, nor is it productive. Let me ask you—do you enjoy hearing others talk about their challenges? Heck no, it can be exhausting, and no one likes to hear it. Yes, we all have emotional needs—to be loved and accepted. But some use negative self-talk to get this attention. They actually make their condition worse (remember, what we think about expands), and this negative attitude only adds more weeds in their mental and physical gardens.

People enjoy being in the presence of fun-loving and uplifting people. So please be very conscious of this—all of the time. Awesome and wonderful words will flow out automatically, and it will be like second nature to you. You will not have to try to speak optimistically— you just will. The negation that one speaks just flows out habitually, without conscious thought. So turn the weeds into wisdom's seeds. Kick that old person out and give your youthfulness a shout. Remember, *the thoughts we think determine whether we swim or sink, and the words we choose determine whether we win or lose.*

CHAPTER TEN

Focus on the Good

When things go wrong, don't go with them.

The good that we focus on makes us healthier and stronger. The negativity and disharmony that we focus on makes us unhealthy and weak. So as you can see, harmony makes us strong and disharmony makes us weak. Praising people when they do things well will go much farther than always criticizing them when they do things that are incorrect in your eyes. Just as darkness is overcome by light, the things people do incorrectly will be overcome by good. What we dwell on is what we become. This is the law of cause and effect in action. When we hear optimistic words praising us and giving us confidence, we feel better about ourselves and want to move forward in life. When we are constantly bombarded by bad self-talk or criticism from others, it is like we are focusing on the weeds in our garden and not the beauty in it. Be most careful of wording things to yourself and to others. Use a calm voice of acceptance, GOODNESS, and harmony, and then watch your gardens grow abundantly; as confidence grows, so will your garden.

I have seen many people who don't want to take responsibility for their challenges. Instead, they look outside themselves for the solutions and answers. The truth lies within them—the challenges started within them—and the solutions lie there also. I have heard so many say, "It is not my fault." Perhaps in some cases this is true, but let's be honest—every time your life is a mess, you are there. Could it be that you made the wrong decisions? Could it be that you chose to take improper action, or no action at all? It is time to own up to your challenges and take responsibility. In order to move forward towards a solution, we need to quit placing blame and speaking words of discord. This will only begin a downward spiral towards a disharmonious existence.

Realize that unhappiness and discord come not from the challenges we face (we all have challenges), but from our perception of them and the way we choose to react to our challenges. The attitude which caused the challenge must be changed into the attitude which is solution-driven. So turn your mind away from the challenge and towards the solution. Quit playing negative mental gymnastics and change your mindset to make it positive. Focus your mind to solution orientation. If you keep your focus on the good, then you will surely bring about much GOODNESS in your world.

CHAPTER ELEVEN

Peace & Health

Focus on the good, and the good grows.

I remember my mom telling me, "If you don't have your health, you don't have anything." Another saying that she used frequently was, "When you're sick, you're not well." Cancer is such a terrible thing. It is a disease that eventually destroys itself; if you think about it, as the bad cells multiply, it then takes its own life because it destroys the house in which it dwells. My mom was so thoughtful. She knew if the experimental surgery didn't help her, then it would help others in the long run. She knew there was an answer to this horrible disease, and because of the courageousness and giving attitude of people like my mom, the answer will be recognized.

Peace and health go hand in hand. I think the more at peace and at ease we are, the less disease can develop. If we take time for health and peace, we won't take so much time for disease and illness. A problem is only a problem if money cannot solve it. If your car engine goes out, it is not really a problem. It may be an inconvenience and not a lot of fun, but it is solvable. You have the option to fix it, get a new engine, or get a different car. If a doctor tells you that you have a challenge where there is no cure—now that is a problem. Invisibly we are perfect, whole, and complete. Some very enlightened people believe we don't have problems in this form—we just think we do. In fact, many believe that enlightenment means an end of suffering.

While seeing my mom go through this experience, I could feel her pain. I remember in the summer of 1995 I had a hernia operation, and it was very painful. I think a veterinarian did the surgery, if I am not mistaken. When I moved wrong and winced, my mom would say, "don't do that." She could feel my pain. At first I thought she may have been kidding, but then I realized she wasn't. Seven years later, while with her in the hospital (she was there for nearly four months), I discovered what she meant. When I saw her in the discomfort and pain she was experiencing, it hurt me so, and I felt pain for my mom. None of us wants to see someone we love so much go through such an experience. It was the absolute worst experience in my world. It even challenged my spiritual beliefs at times. My mom had the courage of an army; the most amazing display of courage I have ever witnessed and probably ever will—and my mom never once complained. Incredible!

When it comes to everyday challenges, perhaps a common sense approach would be to look at the situation and yourself. Put your consciousness in the upper corner of the room and observe yourself and how you are handling the situation. Ask yourself—how will this affect me an hour from now . . . a day from now . . . a week from now . . . a month from now . . . and a year from now?

If it will not affect you in a month or year from now, it is not worth loosing your peace over it. The car engine will get fixed. The secret is not to let the challenge own you and affect your harmony—it's just a bunch of metal, that's all, and money can solve it.

When it comes to getting involved in others' lives, the only time to offer advice ever is never. Getting emotionally involved in others' situations can take our peace away, and most of the time they don't want our advice in the first place. They just want to tell a friend, or eighty-seven of their closest friends, about their challenges. This is not good for several reasons. What we think and talk about expands, so we are literally living the same negative experiences again and again. We experienced and lived it once—why do it eighty-seven more times? Remember, our minds do not know the difference between something that is real in our physical world and something that is imagined in our invisible world. Yesterday ended last night—let it go, it no longer serves you.

I had a friend who was unhappily married for forty years, and she complained relentlessly. Finally she got her wish—a divorce and a ton of money. She was still complaining. I looked at her and said, "You've lived this for forty years and finally got your wish, why would you want to experience your past pain for even forty more seconds—let it go!" This was creating dis-ease in her thoughts, and it will manifest dis-ease in her body if she doesn't start focusing on the good. What we think about expands; so repeat out loud daily (especially while you have perfect health), "Every cell, every fiber of my being is in perfect health." Say to yourself, "I feel great, I look great, and each day in every way I am in perfect health and complete happiness." Tell yourself, "Every cell of my body is in perfect harmony and perfect peace. I live this now. I experience this now and I am grateful for this GOOD now." Our highest GOOD always craves peace. This is the finest gift we can give—our GOODNESS within. Claim your peace now and claim your happiness now—don't wait for it to happen in the future. Hang around with happy and uplifting people. Talk about the good. Read inspirational books and magazines and listen to those types of tapes, CDs, and videos. Don't let negative people and information into your world— they will not help you, they will only hold you back.

A good friend will call his friends on their negativity and not be an enabler—doing so doesn't serve either of you. One thing I've really had to work on is to call people on their "stuff" and have them take responsibility for their words. My friends will tell you—I call them on negative phrases—I reply, "Don't say that. Is that what you want?" Our subconscious minds don't have a sense of humor. We take in what we hear and say, and it is taken literally. I have the attitude of learning not to participate in others' words of discord. I'll be a good listener (if I have to) and wish them well, but I have learned not to have a franchise in their decision to make their problems worse by dwelling on them. I've learned not to offer suggestions most of the time. As mentioned before, they don't want it anyway. If they ask me what they should do, I'll reply, "What do you think you should do?" This gets them to take ownership and responsibility. In other words, to respond with ability. I heard if we would interfere and help a butterfly break free from its cocoon it would not live, because a butterfly gains its strength and muscle from the struggle to break free. Without this process the butterfly would not be able to fly. If we try to help people who are not ready to receive wisdom, then when we are not around they may be lost. Mountains are formed by upheaval. It is always the darkest before the dawn. Sometimes people need to hit rock bottom before they can bounce forward to the next level.

So I am very sensitive and selective with whom I let in my world. Obviously, I would like all of humanity to share these ideas, but people must have the desire to be abundant, happy, and healthy. I have noticed that many people are happy being unhappy. When there is a crisis they become martyrs—they feel best about themselves—yikes. (I think I dated her.) Run from people like that because they'll try to drain your energy. There are plenty of fun and uplifting people. Please spend your time with them.

Most importantly, be very observant of the way you speak to yourself. Always be kind, be gentle, and be patient. I have heard people— rich, wealthy, and "intelligent" people—talk to themselves after they miss a golf shot, and I just can't believe what I am hearing. They call themselves awful names—I'll even learn a few new words from time to time. Never speak to yourself with a negative and self-demeaning phrase. Always speak of the good, think of the good, and treat yourself good. Never belittle yourself. This creates dis-ease and in time you will wish that for every bad statement you had replaced it with a kind, abundant, and loving phrase. Self-talk is crucial when it comes to perfect health, happiness, and peace. You now know what to do. Now go take responsibility for yourself. Be grateful for your health and the gift that we have to live in a country where we can be as abundant as we can believe.

It is not the place in which we live that gives us peace; it is the peace that lives inside of us that puts us in our place. No matter where we go in life, there we are. Sometimes I hear people say that when a situation develops in the future then they'll be okay, at peace, happy, and fulfilled. Well, wanting or waiting to be happy in the future because of moving, changing jobs, getting in a relationship, or getting out of a relationship doesn't matter. The result seems to be consistent. Peace will always be in your future and not in your present. I have always been reflective. I remember twenty-four years ago—I had very little success in others' eyes—yet I was the most successful in my own eyes. By consistently dreaming, taking action, and thinking of creative ways to invent new artistic golf shots, I was on the way to making others smile. Now all I needed was an audience. My dream seed was blooming from an invisible thought into an exciting new visible "thing." In my CONSCIOUS-NESS I had everything that I needed, a goal and the action it took to keep it growing. Being in the moment kept my eyes and heart on bringing smiles to others, not dwelling on my cruddy living arrangements (my kitchen was a refrigerator in the bathroom), and my lack of a social life (owing to my practice schedule). The ability to take my mind off my current situation and have my thoughts remain optimistic and faithful in my calling was, and is, the real success secret for me.

Our current thoughts always determine our future. Putting one's attention on what gives them a happy heart and sharing that happiness can overcome difficult current situations, which will eventually change. I can freely say that I now have so much more in my physical world than I did twenty-four years ago. I have little stress or worry, a secure career, a nice home, and wonderful friends and family—yet I was just as happy on the day that I started my career as I am now. In fact, life was maybe even a bit more exciting back then. My dream seed was in its infancy, growing so quickly, and awesome ideas would pop into my mind all of the time and at the perfect time. A billionaire who lives in a mansion with many servants is not necessarily guaranteed more happiness, peace, and contentment than someone without these things. But having a dream seed, and taking action on it, is what being rich and enjoying inner peace is all about. My mom said to me continuously, "Do your thing, Joey." Bringing happiness to others was, and is, my "thing." It has a wonderful effect, because it took my mind off of me and put it on others. So no matter what was going on in my physical world, I didn't allow it to enter my CONSCIOUSNESS and depress my attitude, because my focus was on others.

One can often be depressed simply by thinking depressed thoughts. One may be unhappy by thinking unhappy thoughts. If we focus on the good in our lives, not the bad, we will be much happier. Like I mentioned before, when my mom had lost her left eye to ocular melanoma, the first thing I remember her saying was, "Others are worse off than I am. Perhaps I can help someone else who is going through this." And she did! My mom's attention wasn't on herself and her eye, it was on giving to others. Never did she complain—incredible. If your world is not that way, and you want it to be, first change that invisible thing called thought—and focus on serving and bringing GOODNESS to others. Get your mind off of you and onto what you can bring to others, not get from them. I believe that this will bring you happiness—it has worked for my mom and for me.

When we dwell on what we don't like, what we don't like will expand in our world. It's just awful fertilizer that is being used unintelligently. Get your mind off this type of thinking. It cannot help you and will not serve you or others. Having that inner peace inside of you is a good start, and will get you out of most any rut. The world is not going to give someone a medal for being a depressed and unhappy martyr. People want to be around uplifting and giving people. So as Emerson respectfully said, "Get your bloated nothingness out of the way." Please, think of my mom's attitude when you get down. Just get over it and move forward, not backward. I often look up in the sky at night, and it makes me realize how insignificant my life's situations really are. Do you realize that there are more stars in the sky than there are pebbles of sand on this earth? Most of our challenges are only a pebble of sand on the road. If we think that our challenges are so big, think again. Although they may seem huge in our little world, they are infantile in the universe. One negative attitude can ruin one's life, yet one awesome idea acted upon can change the world—just ask Henry Ford or the Wright brothers (who were also from Cedar Rapids, Iowa!). The creative ideas that dwell in you are meant to come out and play—so don't delay. Enjoy the place where you are now and put your intention on bringing GOODNESS to others and watch your peaceful garden grow.

AFFIRM OUT LOUD DAILY

- I talk to myself kindly.
- I release all negative people, places, TV programs, and newspaper articles.
- I claim perfect health now, and I share it with others.
- I claim perfect peace now, and I share it with others.
- I claim my perfect life now, and I share it with others.
- I realize if it is to be, it is up to me.
- I know that doing does it.

CHAPTER TWELVE

Value You

Love yourself so much that you are selfless.

I vividly remember when I mistreated a baby frog when I was four years old. My mom, rightfully so, disciplined me and sent me to my room where I cried, looking out the bedroom window seeing other children laugh and play. My mom was teaching me to value life.

One thing I see that puzzles me daily is how people treat and talk to themselves. I don't know one child who would stand on a huge hill and throw his bicycle off a cliff. I don't know one child who would stand on top of his stairs, hold his computer, TV, or stereo above his head and heave it down the stairs, smashing it into a gazillion parts. I don't know one adult who would take his car, set it on a hill, jump out and allow it to smash. And I don't know one person who would take a sledge-hammer and lay his thumb on a table and give it a whack. Yet daily I see people abuse their own bodies by putting things in them that they know aren't healthy. I hear people call themselves names—names they wouldn't say to a stranger—and everyday some people are treating their material possessions with greater care and respect than they give to themselves. This is what mom called, "biting the hand that feeds you." You are not only mistreating yourself, but also all of those around you. It is so illogical that people treat their material possessions with better respect and care than the thing that bought them and brought them home—themselves. Their beautiful minds were the intelligence behind the action (making money) that was needed to obtain the items, and the items are often treated with more reverence than their own minds are.

So the purpose of this chapter is an important one—to start to move you to the top of the list. Make time for yourself and incorporate positivity into your life. If you're mentally, physically, emotionally, and spiritually out of shape—and contributing to it—examine why you are valuing your physical possessions more than your physical body.

AFFIRM OUT LOUD DAILY

- I am a very valuable and worthwhile person.
- I now treat myself with complete care, kindness, and loving GOODNESS.
- I treat my mind, my body, and my emotions with perfect GOODNESS and care.
- No longer do I take better care of my material possessions than I do my own humanity.
- I love myself just the way I am, and each day—in every way—I improve my life, my health, and my self-value.
- I only put good thoughts in my mind and perfect things in my body.
- I know what to do, and I do it.
- Easily and effortlessly, I release all past disharmonious self-beliefs.
- I plant new, wonderful, valuable, and self-appreciating good seeds in my mind, and they grow perfectly.
- Yesterday ended last night, and I effortlessly move forward with self-love and self-respect. I now value myself in totality.

CHAPTER THIRTEEN

Everything Is a Gift If You Believe It Is

To receive love, give love first.

I remember sitting in Mrs. Smith's first grade class crying because she told us to copy down the alphabet, and I could not do it. I was totally confused and frustrated. Reading and phonics were major challenges for me. From then on, I rode my little beat-up black Schwinn bicycle (I loved this bike) to summer school every year for six years straight. My folks sent me to a reading school, but I never got much better. I graduated from Washington High School in Cedar Rapids, Iowa, basically without reading. I took a lot of gym classes, and it brought my grade point average up to probably the 2.0 range—yikes! At the time, I did not know why reading was such a challenge for me. I sure enjoyed writing, and I could use my imagination wonderfully. In fact, when I wrote a story in the eleventh grade (from my own creative thinking), my teacher accused me of plagiarizing.

It was time to go to college, but my SAT and ACT scores were so bad that the University of Iowa wouldn't accept me. They thought it would be best to go to a junior college for a year and then see what progress I had made. I guess my SAT reading score of a whopping 2 wasn't quite good enough! (You would think that randomly filling in circles would result in a score better than a 2; I couldn't even guess well.) It was probably the worst score in the history of the world, and I'm still proud of that record. After a year at Kirkwood Community College, I was doing well in math, and the following year the University of Iowa accepted me. It was very frustrating for me. I remember going to a teacher for help, and he said, "I don't have time for rotten students, and Son, you're a rotten student." Well, he was correct, but I knew that I was a good person. I still couldn't read a book unless it was a golf book, and even then I couldn't comprehend a thing or stay focused long enough to hardly get through a paragraph. So by my senior year—after the three most frustrating years of my life—I quit buying the books. They were nothing but a waste of money to me. But I did grant my dad's wish and got that diploma from the University of Iowa without reading a lick. I believe my diploma is the Eighth Wonder of the world. About twelve years later, I decided to improve my reading skills. To make a long story short, a doctor told me he felt that I had not one, but two forms of dyslexia and ADHD. So I'm one of the few people who will have written more books than they have read!

It turns out that this challenge was, and is, a beautiful gift because I have used my intelligence in a way to live and lead my life happily and with fulfillment. I have focused on bringing GOODNESS to humanity ever since my folks took me to a circus at four years of age, and now I do exactly that. No one is good at everything, but we are all good at something, and the secret is to find that something and use it to bring GOODNESS to ourselves and to share that GOODNESS with others. Imagine this—I make my living hitting golf balls off a six-foot unicycle and balancing upside down on one hand while hitting a golf ball with the other. The smartest people in my high school may not like their jobs as much as I do. I love mine in totality, and most people could read circles around me. Intelligence is doing what you love and loving what you do. I know millionaire executives who do not like their jobs. They travel here and there, constantly being pulled and pushed by meetings and people. They have lots of money, but their work is stressful, and their occupations own them. There is a difference between standard of living and quality of life. Never let your job own you; have control over your time. Find what you love, sell that love for your "job," and go play to make your living. That is a gift—enjoying your life at work, as well as at home.

You wonder how I can hit a golf ball off a six-foot unicycle.
I wonder how you can read.

CHAPTER FOURTEEN

The Dishwasher Lesson Can Work For You, Too

The secret to being happy is to be a happy being.

It seems that every time I empty the dishwasher, I am reminded of a profound lesson that my mom taught me. As I remove the dishes and silverware, I can vividly still hear my mom telling me, "If you would just do it and stop talking about how much you dislike doing it, you'd have it done already and could go outside and play." As a little boy, one of my responsibilities was to empty the dishwasher. My mom was teaching me then, and even today in CONSCIOUSNESS, that doing does it. Getting your mind off a disharmonious or boring task and putting it on something fun, creative, and exciting is the way to go. As I look back on things that weren't enjoyable for me, I realize that I applied my mom's wisdom often. When I drove to California from Iowa it seemed like it took forever, and when I finally arrived I slept in my car in the Howard Johnson's parking lot. Boy, was I brave! (Or was I na ve? Okay, both.) The next night I upgraded to a couch. But after that I downsized to a chair in the golf shop at Lakeside Country Club, where I slept for the next six weeks. All the time I was putting my attention on my dream seeds of giving happiness and off the "dishwasher." I was doing exactly what my mom had taught me fifteen years prior. It worked then and works still today.

Becoming productive each day is so much fun. Real accomplishment and doing things that others find difficult is so rewarding. It also gives you peace and confidence. Words of wisdom from Earl Nightingale affirm that one of the best ways to get things accomplished is to list, before going to bed, all of the goals you have for the next day. Let's say there are ten items on the list. After listing them, re-list them in the order of importance of getting them accomplished. Start each morning with item number one, and complete it. Do not go on to item number two until number one is complete. Even if item number one takes you hours, finish it. Work (or play) your way through the list and get as many items done (hopefully all of them) as possible.

You'll be amazed how your garden of abundance grows, and you won't find the time to pay attention to any "weeds" in your life. Do this everyday for a month, and you will be so happy with your productivity level that you will make these lists for the rest of your life. My two dream seeds that I nurture daily are to make perfect use of time and to be better than the previous day. Discover your dream seeds, list the actions that are needed to achieve them, and go for it. *Go the extra mile; this will make you smile.* Commit to this! Just do this!

CHAPTER FIFTEEN

If You Can Dream It, You Can Do It

Limitless thoughts produce limitless results.

Although it was about forty-two years ago, I remember it like yesterday. At age four, my mom and dad took me to the circus in my home state of Iowa, and on that day I planted and knew that I wanted to be an entertainer—I wanted to make people laugh. (I also wanted a job where I could wear shorts and tennis shoes to work, and I have it.) I believe having this "knowingness" at age four was really a gift, which I am so grateful for. Many young people may have a dream seed at a young age, and it becomes lost. Perhaps a well-meaning person said something negative about that dream to the young person, and the child let it go. The more bizarre the dream seed is, the more attainable it may be. This is because these unique ideas are so pure and come from within at such a precious age. Well, it sure worked for me, and I hope I can be an example.

We are never too old or too young to plant a wonderful thought (dream seed). Our invisible CONSCIOUSNESS does not know age as a number and it does not care. It is our attitude towards our age that is more important. If we can imagine something, then we can do it. We just need to take action; we need to physically and mentally do what it takes to fertilize and help the growth process of our dream seed.

I also remember, quite vividly, a discussion that my mom and I shared at a young age. I wanted the time and days to pass quickly because I was excited for the upcoming weekend. I said, "I can't wait until Saturday, I want it to hurry up and be here now!" My mom replied, "Joey, never wish your life away. A day gone is gone forever, and it cannot come back. Enjoy each day and make it the best you can. Then you will have a life that is happy and full." I could not have received a more profound gift of wisdom.

My mother realized that I had a unique gift. Although I often did not see what most others see (I was quite na ve), I did have a knack for seeing what most do not see at all. I had an incredible dream, and I would achieve it. I chose role models such as the great Ben Hogan. He was not only the finest golf ball striker in his day, but he was also a wonderful user of that invisible gift of time. I am so grateful that I not only listened to my mom and dad's wisdom, but I also took action on it and applied it to my life. That is the key for me.

As I mentioned, I have two goals daily—to make perfect use of my time each day and to be better than I was the day before. The cumulative effect of this has amazing results, similar to compounding interest. Was it Einstein who said compounding interest is one of the most incredible things he has ever witnessed? I believe it was. Speaking of Einstein, I really enjoy his saying, "Great spirits have always encountered violent opposition from mediocre minds."

I took the liberty of adding a word to this for ol' Albert, "Great spirits have always encountered violent opposition from mediocre *use* of minds." You see, we are all given a mind but some of us choose to use it with mediocrity. Our minds are not average. Our minds are always used brilliantly. The true question is—are they used brilliantly for abundance? What we plant in our CONSCIOUSNESS and take action on will manifest in our physical world if we truly focus on it. So what are you planting and cultivating?

My mom always encouraged me to "do your thing." I practiced so much, even as a small boy. In the winter I would shovel some snow away in the front yard and go outside and practice in any and all weather conditions. (Iowa had some pretty intense weather at times.) My mom knew I had a personality that was better at creating rather than competing. I would expect the very most out of myself. Very little could interrupt my drive (no pun intended) and my practice schedule. I would practice until my hands would literally bleed. The calluses on my hands were so profound that even when I didn't have a golf club in my hands, they were formed like I did. I would practice in the gym, too. In fact, when I was learning how to do hand stands and back flips, my teachers would put thumbtacks on the floor below me on the parallel bars—so I learned to hold on pretty quickly. I remember when I ripped my stomach muscles learning back flips, I would scream in pain if I moved the wrong way (or moved at all). I was still the first one on the practice tee in the morning, and always the last one off at night. Ben Hogan would have been proud of me.

The reason I share these stories is to express that "doing your thing" can take tremendous discipline—far more discipline than talent. My mom once told me that I was the only one in the family with discipline. She loved how I would stand up for myself. Sometimes she had to tell me to tone it down and remember to be nice. I will always remember the last show that my mom attended; she was as excited as she was at her first show. To see her smile and clap was the greatest gift I have ever received. Even now, before I go to sleep at night, I say out loud, "Thank you, Ma. Love you, Ma!" This story is a tearful one for me to write and share with others. I am constantly CONSCIOUS of my mom; I have her initials (P.A.N.O.) on my shirts and visors.

My mom once asked me if I felt I was a genius. I am sure I hesitated and answered, "Probably so—we are all geniuses." I know when it came to school that I was not even close to genius status. But when it comes to "doing my thing" and living my life exactly how I want to live it—then I feel ingenious.

PART THREE | AFFIRMATION

CHAPTER SIXTEEN

What Is an Affirmation?

Wisdom is knowledge in action.

An affirmation is a movement of spoken and enthusiastic words with an end result in mind. A good way to help visualize these ideas in your imagination is through the use of posters and collages. You must have a total belief that what you seek is already yours in your mind—your invisible world. Affirmations also help you recognize this truth about yourself, and this truth will set you free of any doubt, fear, or confusion.

Positive affirmation work moves you to your HIGHEST GOOD, so you can bring GOODNESS to others as well. Remember always to use harmonious and positive words in affirmations. Never use a negative word in a positive affirmation. Our minds don't have a sense of humor, and they take negative words literally. If I said to you, "Don't think of Bozo the clown," you would picture Bozo the clown. So say what you want, picture it, and produce it in your world. This is so very important and works beautifully as you stay focused on what you want and turn away from what you do not want. Also know that we are always creating affirmations in our lives, so be careful about using negative words throughout the day. If someone asks you how you are, don't ever say "not bad;" by saying that, you will have just used two negative words that are, in essence, negative affirmations in your consciousness. Just say that you are perfect, even if you may not feel perfect at that second. If you say it long enough, you start to believe it and live it. Also be careful how you word other sentences. Instead of, "Don't let me forget," say, "Please remind me." This is more affirmative and tells the subconscious mind a more positive way of demonstrating your GOOD.

Our conscious minds are our daily thoughts. I like to compare it to the captain of a ship. The captain tells the crew what to do. The crew is similar to our subconscious mind. Whatever the captain (conscious mind) says, the crew (subconscious mind) always says *yes*. The subconscious mind never says *no* and has no sense of humor. If you verbally say, "I feel horrible today," you will feel horrible because your subconscious mind will allow this. The crew is only taking directions from the captain to feel horrible. What you say, feel, and think in your mental world will be demonstrated in your physical world. So this is why it is so crucial always to word your sentences and express them verbally in an affirmative and positive way, using only positive words.

Also, visualize and picture the results you wish for. For example, if you are overweight and would like to lose weight, picture yourself at your ideal weight. This training of your conscious mind will bring positive results in your physical world. Correct words and pictures can, and will, dramatically change the way you reach your dream seeds. If we say or picture things in the future, they will always be in the future, and we will never get to demonstrate them in the present. If you say, "I am going to lose fifty pounds," you will always be going to lose fifty pounds. You should say, "I can see in my mind and feel right now my body fifty pounds lighter. I am at my correct and perfect weight right now." Get a picture from a magazine with the body that you want and put your face over theirs and look at it often.

This training of your conscious daily words will dramatically train your subconsciousness to lead you towards your goals. So say it as already so, picture it as already so, and be patient and open to wonderful ideas. You will receive invisible gifts, even when you least expect them, so be open and take action on any and all hunches and ideas you receive from your inner wisdom. This wisdom is your subconsciousness directing you to your dream seed and helps the conscious mind grow abundantly.

CHAPTER SEVENTEEN

Daily Affirmations

POSITIVE AFFIRMATION FOR
FINDING THE RIGHT RELATIONSHIP

I, ____, affirm these words out loud many times daily. The good I am looking for is looking for me. I now claim this union with my perfect mate. My mate is happy, honest, and healthy. We share the same values and morals. All that I desire in this beautiful relationship I am also willing to give. We support and nurture each other. Effortlessly, we share our love! It is this love that allows us to accept each other in totality. I give grateful thanks for this GOODNESS to share. I affirm and know it is so.

SEEDS OF WISDOM

POSITIVE AFFIRMATION FOR
KEEPING MARRIAGE HAPPY & LASTING

I, _____, affirm these words out loud many times daily. My marriage is filled with love, harmony, and peace. I look for the good in this beautiful relationship, and I compliment my spouse daily. Each day, in every way, our love grows stronger. Our relationship is built on honesty and trust. It is filled with love, passion, and excitement. I am so grateful for my wonderful spouse. I give grateful thanks for this GOODNESS to share. I affirm and know it is so.

POSITIVE AFFIRMATION FOR
RELEASING A MATERIAL OBJECT (e.g., a house)

I, ____, affirm these words out loud many times daily. The good I am looking for is looking for me. My home has served me well. It is now time to release it to someone who can enjoy it as much as I have. I release this home in the perfect time and at the perfect price. I am grateful for this honest and harmonious transaction. I give grateful thanks for this GOODNESS to share. I affirm and know it is so.

POSITIVE AFFIRMATION FOR
THE DECISION OF PEACE

I, ____, affirm these words out loud many times daily. I now choose peace! I release all disharmonious people, places, and things in my world. I accept calm and joy. I accept others' ways of life, even if they differ from mine. I tend to my garden, and this gives me peace. No one can upset me without my permission. I now claim control over my thoughts. I accept ownership in this freedom and rejoice in this truth. I give grateful thanks for this GOODNESS to share. I affirm and know it is so.

POSITIVE AFFIRMATION FOR
THE PERFECT WEIGHT

I, ____, affirm these words out loud many times daily. I now see myself at my ideal weight. Wow, I feel great and look terrific! I now respond with ability. I put the perfect food in my mouth and the perfect thoughts in my mind. I believe in myself. I have total control over what I allow into my body; food no longer owns me. I am guided to the perfect people who help me reach my goal of ____ pounds or lighter. I love myself. I enjoy my life. Each day, in every way, I am healthier, lighter, stronger, and more energized. My life works beautifully. I move freely and effortlessly. I know what to do and I do it. I give grateful thanks for this GOODNESS to share. I affirm and know it is so.

POSITIVE AFFIRMATION FOR
ENERGY

I, _____, affirm these words out loud many times daily. I am abundant energy in action. I love life and life loves me. Each day, in every way, I enthusiastically move forward. Wow, my life is awesome. I surround myself with fun-loving, energetic people. I speak, think, and act with incredible energy. I am filled with optimism. I release all negative thoughts, feelings, and actions. Low energy no longer serves me. I move forward with gusto. I am healthy, vibrant, alert, and alive. My world is awesome. I give grateful thanks for this GOODNESS to share. I affirm and know it is so.

POSITIVE AFFIRMATION FOR
CREATIVE IMAGINATION

I, ____, affirm these words out loud many times daily. I now use my intelligence intelligently. Awesome, creative ideas flow through me effortlessly. I take action on them. I demonstrate them. These ideas are fun and exciting. I bring goodness to humanity daily. My ideas grow abundantly and brilliantly. Perfect ideas always come to me at the perfect time and place. My creative imagination is alert, alive, and awake. I listen to my inner voice. My highest good is demonstrated beautifully with joy. I give grateful thanks for this GOODNESS to share. I affirm and know it is so.

POSITIVE AFFIRMATION FOR
BEING A BETTER LISTENER

I, ____, affirm these words out loud many times daily. I listen perfectly. I look into others' eyes as they speak. I allow them to complete their sentences. I have two ears and one mouth for a reason; I listen twice as much as I speak. When I speak, I learn little. When I listen, I learn very much. I listen so well that I hear all words and the meaning behind the words. I release the need to interrupt. I release the need to be right. I release the need to be heard.

I listen to my inner voice as well. I take action on my wonderful invisible hunches. My mind is open and receptive. My listening skills improve daily, my life improves daily. I accept and give this wonderful gift of listening. I give grateful thanks for this GOODNESS to share. I affirm and know it is so.

POSITIVE AFFIRMATION FOR
INTEGRITY & HONESTY

I, ____, affirm these words out loud many times daily. My word is my bond. I am honest to all, myself included. I mean what I say and I say what I mean. My word is impeccable. My life is integrity in action. I treat others as I wish to be treated. My standards are high, and I use them for the highest good for all. I do things correctly the first time. The quality of my work for others is as good as if I were doing it for myself. I walk my walk, I talk my talk. I am what I am. Honesty and integrity are the seeds in my garden, and they grow perfectly daily. I give grateful thanks for this GOODNESS to share. I affirm and know it is so.

POSITIVE AFFIRMATION FOR
REMAINING YOUTHFUL ALWAYS

I, _____, affirm these words out loud many times daily. I now affirm youthfulness. I think young, I act young, and I feel young. My spirit is alert, alive, and awake. Age is an attitude, not a number. I effortlessly remove old thinking from my consciousness. I am here to love life and experience good, and I do. I only allow uplifting, positive thoughts in my mind. My words are affirmative. I spend time with positive people with youthful attitudes. Age is no longer an excuse. My body feels great, and I move freely with ease. My memory and mind function perfectly. I smile more. I laugh more. I share my excitement for life with all. My youthful spark is contagious. People love me, and I love people. My voice resonates excitement. My step has a spring to it. I am filled with youthful vitality and energy. I give grateful thanks for this GOODNESS to share. I affirm and know it is so.

POSITIVE AFFIRMATION FOR
TIME & TIMING

I, _____, affirm these words out loud many times daily. I use my twenty-four hours productively. Each day, in every way, my growth is abundant. I am filled with optimism and trust. I am action in motion. I listen to my hunches. I am grateful for these gifts. Effortlessly, I tune in to my consciousness and accept information freely. Perfect ideas are revealed at the perfect time and place. Everything is in perfect order and synch with nature's laws. I allow things to unfold in nature's time. I force nothing. I am led. I am shown. I am directed. My timing is perfect. I remain relaxed. I grow to my fullest daily. I know all is on time, every time, in my world. I give grateful thanks for this GOODNESS to share. I affirm and know it is so.

POSITIVE AFFIRMATION FOR
FORGIVING & LETTING GO

I, ____, affirm these words out loud many times daily. Yesterday ended last night. Today I begin a new day. I release all negative experiences, people, and things that no longer serve me. I release negative thoughts and emotions from past experiences. I let them go! I send forgiveness to all, and in doing so I release their control over me. I allow self-healing to occur. I am healed. I release all needs to judge and to control. I am tolerant, and I accept the differences in all people. I honor and accept my uniqueness, and I respect the uniqueness in others. My attention is in the moment. My future is filled with optimism. I am harmony and love in action. I live and let live. I give grateful thanks for this GOOD-NESS to share. I affirm and know it is so.

POSITIVE AFFIRMATION FOR
THE PERFECT OCCUPATION

I, ____, affirm these words out loud many times daily. The perfect job that I am looking for is looking for me. We now meet! I am a wonderful employee. I give one hundred percent. I love what I do, and I do what I love. This opportunity rewards me with the perfect amount of money, benefits, and hours. Easily I can support my family and myself. My employer treats me perfectly. We are a perfect fit. Each day I go to work with enthusiasm and joy. I grow and learn daily. I bring goodness to all. I give grateful thanks for this GOODNESS to share. I affirm and know it is so.

CHAPTER EIGHTEEN

How to Write an Affirmation

Happiness has to be thought.

1. Get into a quiet, peaceful state of mind.
2. Write down your intention, or what you desire, on the top of the page.
3. Know and believe that this will also bring GOODNESS to others. Write that down, too.
4. Write down a sentence or short paragraph and claim your union with that which you desire (e.g., peace, happiness, fulfillment, love, success). Capitalize these words.
5. Write down and claim that what you want is already here now, in this present moment. (You don't say you want perfect health. You claim that you are in perfect health now, even if you don't feel it now.)
6. Denial option—write down a sentence or two releasing the negation or lack that you are overcoming. (For example, "I release all fear, all doubt, all obstacles, and all negation.")
7. Always use positive and optimistic words in your affirmations except

if you choose to use the denial option. Never use phrases like "I'm going to," "In the future," or, "I hope." Use phrases like "I claim," "I declare," and, "I now accept." Also, never use questions. Write your affirmation in the present tense as if it already so.

8. Always express your gratitude for this GOODNESS in every affirmation. Read it out loud as many times daily as needed, until you see the realization in your physical world. Sometimes it truly helps if you can walk in nature when doing affirmations. Commit affirmations to memory.

9. Know the truth about you—you are perfect and awesome just the way you are. Write that down and claim it, know it, feel it, accept it, and visualize it.

10. Let it go and "water" it every day with correct thinking, visualizing, and verbally confirming it to be so.

CHAPTER NINETEEN

Creating Your Affirmative
Dream Seed Vision Book

You're only as good as your preparation.

What you will need:

1. A three ring notebook
2. Numerous clear plastic inserts for a three ring notebook
3. A vision of what you desire
4. An imagination

Creating a dream seed vision book is fun and rewarding. You can get creative on a typewriter (if they are still around) or a computer. Make 8" x 10" posters of what you want, and include personal photographs, magazine pages and pictures, and any other personal effects.

For example, if you desire a well-defined stomach, then cut out pictures of this from magazines and paste your face to the body. This creates a vision of your goal and makes it easier to visualize. Put an affirmation on the sheet, "This is my stomach now." Make sure you write your affirmations as though the goal is already met.

Include as many sheets (or visions) as you would like in your book. You could design one for relationship goals, business goals, financial goals, health goals, etc. Look at your book daily and affirm your goals. Keep this book near your bed and look at it before going to sleep at night. The dream seeds will then be in your subconscious mind as you rest. The invisible will begin to manifest in your physical world. Allow the dream seeds to grow in nature's time—not in your time—and just do your best daily. You will see results in no time.

CHAPTER TWENTY

Harvest Time

The whole key to life is to use your intelligence intelligently.

On some level, I often wonder if we do make the decision to be born and the decision to pass on. It is so difficult when the people we love make this transition, because they may be ready to go, but we want them to stay. Honoring their decision to pass is often so very difficult. I've heard that we are never more alive than the minute we take our last breath. I don't know for sure, but I wouldn't be surprised if this is so. My body literally shook, and I cried as my mom took her final breath. Although I knew she was ready to release this form and move on, it was such a difficult experience. To know that we will all leave this form is a profound thought to grasp. I believe that our thoughts will continue on, and thank you, Mom, for so many beautiful loving lessons, moments, and memories. Whether we are on this planet for eight days or eighty-eight years, in universal time it is a mere blink. I think we should be grateful for what we have, and even be grateful for what we do not have. The way my mother lived, the way she always gave selflessly to humanity, has never ceased to amaze me. I am thankful for the awesome and beautiful role model that she was, and still is today. Even in her final days, Mom gave her life and body so a cure would be found; what a wonderful human being my mom was. I am truly proud to be her son.

I know that we are one together in CONSCIOUSNESS, and I look forward to seeing my mom again. We'll be sharing our smiles and hugs. I was told to never put a question mark where our CREATOR puts a period. Well, after a period begins a new sentence, a new beginning. Just like water evaporates and returns to it source in the sky above, it returns again to experience its time on earth over and over. Knowing what this book is all about—that what we think about expands—I have put into mind the gift of being with my mom again, and I know it will be great fun. Yet in the meantime, being one in CONSCIOUSNESS, I'll continue living my life the way my ma did and would want me to—giving, receiving, sharing, smiling, and knowing that our time on earth is "only a hobby."

It's only a hobby, so enjoy it. Speak of the good, look for the good, share your GOODNESS and keep on planting the GOODNESS that you are. Keep the fertilizer going, and your life will be growing. I hope you think of and are inspired by my mom from time to time and have gotten to know her well and received her awesome gifts. "It's only a hobby." I love you, Mom!

My Beloved Mom, Pat.

1932 - 2003

This was the letter that was read
during my mom's funeral service . . .

Dear Ma,

I know you are safe and at peace now; this gives me great comfort, although I am so sad, cry much, and miss you so. The courage you showed was the greatest I will ever witness, and the pain you endured—mentally, emotionally, physically, and spiritually—was too much for an entire army. I could feel it in every fiber of my being and had trouble handling it; I did my best and will always be truly amazed at how well you handled it all. These last two and a half weeks (being with you) were so emotional, and I honored every moment with you. It was truly a wonderful gift. I reflected on how much you shared, taught, and showed me—by both actions and with words—and how you handled all situations. I always knew you were incredibly wise and strong, yet these past days I reflected so much on the past forty-five years being in your presence and realized I owe so much to you for you sharing your wisdom. I know you want me to get over my grieving and begin to be productive again, and I will do my best for you. Perhaps today people will have a renewed awareness about life and the livingness of your gifts.

Children are given the gift of life from their mothers; yet, the greater gift is to be an example for that child on how to live that gift to its fullest. Ma, you did, you taught me well. I know you're proud, I can hear you saying now, "Live and let live" and "It's only a hobby." Your incredible ability to focus on the solution to the challenge, instead of the challenge itself, is one of the secrets to this existence. I know you knew this, and I am so grateful and honored that you demonstrated it time after time. You knew that what we think about expands, what we dwell upon we become, and what we think about we bring about. When I hear people complain about the littlest scrape or pain, I immediately think of your courage and wisdom. You always focused on the good and never complained. Your attitude of mind and words was, and is, truly an example for every spiritual being. You've sure made my world a better place by your example of true spirit, true hope, and planting GOODNESS and pulling the weeds of worry, disharmony, and discord from your mental garden before they could grow. You did this brilliantly for seventy-one years. We will always be one in CONSCIOUSNESS, and I can now feel and hear your guidance, and this gives me great strength and comfort and peace.

Know I am your biggest fan, and I will even put more effort into becoming an even better person, like you. I appreciate you letting me know you're okay from time to time. In fact, I saw two cardinals today, and they seemed so cheery and looked so beautiful—just like you, Ma. Thank you for that gift. You're the best giver in the world, and the gifts you shared with me in your last hours here were the best and most memorable ever—the kiss on the cheek, the holding of hands, and the looks in our eyes with your special tears. I will always cherish these moments in my heart. I couldn't have wished for any finer or more special gifts, and I thank you for those gifts, as I knew the energy it must have taken.

Keep 'em smiling in heaven, Ma, and I'll use your wisdom to keep 'em smiling down here. I know "it's only a hobby" down here, and together we can keep God smiling, too. I will always love you with every fiber of my soul.

Love, your son Joey

THE BEGINNING.

THE DREAM SEED SERIES®

Available at Amazon.com

The Dream Seed (Paperback)

Seeds of Wisdom: A Son's Promise Kept (Trade Paperback)

VHS & DVDs available directly through Joey O:

The Dream Seed (Educational VHS/DVD)

Picture Perfect Golf (Instructional VHS/DVD)

Joey O Show (Entertainment VHS/DVD)

For additional information, to order Joey O's books and videos, or
to schedule entertainment or speaking, please contact:

Joey O

PO Box 1196

Cedar Rapids, Iowa 52406-1196

Telephone (319) 365-7546 Ext. 302

Large quantity discounts are available for schools,
churches, and organizations.